Sophie Dugueyt

Psychometrics. Quick review

GRIN Verlag

Bibliografische Information der Deutschen Nationalbibliothek:

Die Deutsche Bibliothek verzeichnet diese Publikation in der Deutschen National-
bibliografie; detaillierte bibliografische Daten sind im Internet über http://dnb.d-
nb.de/ abrufbar.

Imprint:

Copyright © 2011 GRIN Verlag GmbH
Druck und Bindung: Books on Demand GmbH, Norderstedt Germany
ISBN: 978-3-656-55852-1

This book at GRIN:

http://www.grin.com/en/e-book/266009/psychometrics-quick-review

During the course, we had the opportunity to discover the psychometrics. This overview demonstrated the importance of business psychology as it helps to work more efficiently and to have a better understanding of people's behavior. Psychometrics is used to define and to analyze human characteristics and it is often applied at a business level. We studied several methods which can be useful to improve individuals' work performances and the atmosphere within a company. It is an important tool to compose effective teams, to detect people's capabilities and to find efficient leaders. Thanks to these analyses, one can also be more capable to find employees who perfectly suit one's company and one's sector. In fact, a "psychological" selection is frequently employed in addition to interviews to reveal the real personality of an applicant.

However, psychometrics can also be useful at a personal level. Indeed, it enables someone to understand himself or herself better, what they really are inside and what their personality really is. Moreover, it can contribute to make better choices and decisions for a future life, for a career. Thanks to these tests, you can decide which work position suits you best and which team member type you are.

First, I will give my opinion regarding the individual side of psychometrics, looking at how it can be contribute to in our daily life. Then, I will study the business level psychometrics with its strengths and weaknesses.

To begin with, psychometrics is an important tool to understand who you are and what your personality really is. Thanks to this tool, you are able to define your strengths and your weaknesses. Actually, you understand what your behavior results from, according to tests which evaluate your personality or your intelligence. For instance, the Myers and Briggs Type Indicator gives you an accurate profile according to specialists. As far as I am concerned, I am of the opinion that your personality can change during your life and that you can have different answers according to the periods, events or experiences you are going through. As I suggested during the course, in the MBTI, you have to choose between two proposals and there is a question about if you prefer building or structure. I think that when you are young and growing, you will take the first answer because you are in the optic of building your future life whereas if you are older and a mother more exactly, you will probably tend to answer structure because you need strong bases in this new life. I am quite sure that your personality is changing all the time because you are learning from your experiences and errors.

Then, we can suppose that psychometrics can help you in your choice for your future career. In fact, thanks to these tests, you can have typical jobs which are recommended for your kind of personality. Even if it doesn't tell you what you have to do, they give you clues to succeed in a field that corresponds to your personality. In this sense, you are able to exploit your competences and to be happier with your job. Moreover, you can realize your strengths and weaknesses and you know what you have to work on to improve and which part of your personality needs efforts. Nonetheless, as the specialists say, the lists of jobs that are supposed to suit you are not exhaustive and you can be perfectly competent in another sector. For example, my MBTI revealed I should be a comedian but as the professor said, I can do whatever I want if I fight for it. I think I can learn to suit perfectly to a certain type of job. Actually, I believe that humans are "adaptable", meaning that they can cope with situations they are not used to or comfortable with. It is important to notice that you can change and get more competences in any situation. For instance, in business schools, you have to do many oral presentations and even if you are an introvert, you get use to this exercise and you can even be good at it with time.
After this personal "analysis", we can think about the value of psychometrics at work and how it helps employers to evaluate you depending if you are suitable to a certain job position.

On the one hand, psychometrics, and more exactly the MBTI, can be very useful to choose among many applicants. One has to recognize the usefulness of this tool in finding the right person for a job position, regarding his or her abilities to complete the functions for that particular job position. For example, if you need to meet customers or if you have to make conferences, it is better to be an extravert. The employer can take an ideal decision according to the characteristics of the job. It is as well a good way to create a strong team as it builds a complementary team. It is an advantage to mix characteristics and skills among employees. The MBTI can give the employer the opportunity to take the perfect employee who will easily integrate the existing team. The manager can realize that his team will be more performing with a new personality for example. Moreover, it is a good solution to understand the others because a manager will know how to react according to the personality of the person he faces. Actually, thanks to the MBTI he will be able to manage conflicts more easily as he will understand how to explain things and how to solve the problems according to the different personalities. He will be able to adapt to the different types and can thus be clearer. Then, a manager can decide to employ a person who is more or less like him to avoid conflicts. In fact, it can be a good idea to hire somebody similar to you because that person will know your reactions, your ways of doing.

I think that these tests are used in many different businesses and it shows if you are able to do your job efficiently or not. For instance, the NASA (see appendix) and the Police always use "psychological" tests to be sure the applicant will correspond to the mission he or she will be given. In the NASA case, the company is checking if the future employee will have the good reaction in a dangerous situation because the job needs somebody who reacts rapidly and copes with pressure. For the Police entry tests, it is more to find out if you are motivated and if you tend to be a murderer (for instance, if you will kill someone with your weapon).

On the other hand, I think that psychometrics can be source of "discrimination". In fact, human resources will try to find the perfect type of personality for a job and they will only concentrate on applicants with the perfect type. They will have to answer the MBTI test before the interview and will not care about their experiences and competences. I think it can become a problem, because as I suggested before, you can change during your life because your previous experiences can modify your personality, so one can always learn to adapt for a particular job.

When all is said and done, I believe that managers need to make a difference between personal and professional life. You cannot be judged on you personality because you can pretend to be someone else at work and be yourself at home. As long as you are working well, I do not see why your personality should interfere in your professional life.

To conclude, I think psychometrics is a useful tool to determine the personality and it can help you to make choices for your future career. It is also an advantage for employers as they are able to find a person who perfectly suits the job. However, I maintain that there is an evolution in our life and that the MBTI is not always accurate and what is more, it can even be discriminatory at work.